KNOWING GOD'S LOVE

KNOWING GOD'S LOVE

VISIONS FROM HEAVEN

SUSAN SINN

Knowing God's Love
Published by Susan Sinn
with Castle Publishing

© 2021 Susan Sinn
Australia

ISBN 978-0-6453397-0-3 (Softcover)
ISBN 978-0-6453397-1-0 (ePUB)
ISBN 978-0-6453397-2-7 (Kindle)

Editing: Andrea Candy

Production & Typesetting:
Lizelle Windon & Andrew Killick
Castle Publishing Services
www.castlepublishing.co.nz

Cover Design:
Paul Smith

Unless otherwise stated, scriptures are taken from
the Holy Bible, New International Version®, NIV®.
Copyright © 1973, 1978, 1984, 2011 by Biblica, Inc.™
Used by permission of Zondervan.
All rights reserved worldwide.

ALL RIGHTS RESERVED

No part of this publication may be reproduced,
stored in a retrieval system, or transmitted
in any form or by any means, electronic, mechanical,
photocopying, recording or otherwise,
without prior written permission from the author.

Contents

1. The Love of Jesus — 9
2. The Father's Love — 11
3. The Trinity — 15
4. My Story — 19
5. God's Love Covenant — 23
6. God Makes Us a New Creation — 29
7. God Gives Us Gifts — 33
8. God's Plans for Us — 43
9. Resting in the Victory of Christ Jesus — 49
10. Unite and Fight — 57
11. The Weapon of Peace — 63
12. The Weapon of Love — 67
13. The Weapon of Signs and Wonders — 71
14. The Weapon of Perseverance — 77
15. The Weapon of Praise — 81
16. The Weapon of Sowing and Reaping — 87
17. Our Words Have Power — 91
18. Knowing God's Love — 95

Arise, my dearest. Hurry, my darling.
    Come away with me!
    I have come as you have asked
    to draw you to my heart and lead you out.
    For now is the time, my beautiful one.
                           (Song of Songs 2:10 TPT)

Chapter 1
THE LOVE OF JESUS

In a vision, I asked Jesus, "What was it like on the cross?"

His response was one word – "Horrendous."

I then asked Him, "So why did you do it?"

He said, "I was compelled by my love for you."

This book is all about God's love for us. It is something that can be hard to comprehend. Paul realised this and prayed the following prayer:

> I pray that you, being rooted and established in love, may have power, together with all the Lord's holy people, to grasp how wide and long and high and deep is the love of Christ, and to know this love that surpasses knowledge – that you may be filled to the measure of all the fullness of God.
>
> (Ephesians 3:17-19)

It appears from this that we don't automatically grasp the love of Christ! I know I didn't. I only started to grasp how much He loved me when I was 39. It was when I woke up one morning blown away by the realisation of what Jesus dying on the cross really meant in terms of what He had done for me.

A couple of years after this, I had a vision and in it I was suspended in the air above a body of water. I could see the sunlight sparkling on the water below. I remember feeling happy and pretty good about myself.

However, then I heard the devil (Satan) say to me, "Who do you think you are, you miserable little worm?" It was as though he spoke the words right into my ear.

Those words instantly had the effect of making me acutely aware of all my faults and shortcomings. It was a horrible, overwhelming sensation which made me feel weak and despairing. I felt I wasn't even good enough to be compared to a worm.

As a result, I felt myself falling into the water. Then I could feel Satan pushing me down under the water. I couldn't breathe and I realised I was drowning. In my depressed state, that seemed OK as I didn't think I deserved to live. Also in that tormented space, I rationalised that my loved ones would be better off without me and wondered if anyone would care if I died. It was almost a relief to know that the end was near and I wouldn't have to put up with the torment anymore.

However, I then felt myself being pulled up out of the water. Someone had put their hands under my armpits and was pulling me out of the water and onto dry land.

Once on the land, I felt the most wonderful sensation of love and warmth enveloping me. I opened my eyes and saw that the person who had saved me was Jesus.

He looked at me and His first words to me were, "I care. I care so much, I died for you and I love you regardless."

Jesus had refuted Satan's lies – someone did care – it was Him, He always cares. His love is that encompassing.

Those experiences were the beginning of grasping God's love for me. However, I still had a way to go.

Chapter 2
THE FATHER'S LOVE

Love was chasing me and I didn't realise it. I was terrified. It was my heavenly Father chasing me. He had the appearance of a tall clean-shaven man in his early thirties. I was running away as fast as I could, because I was scared of what would happen if He caught me. I was anticipating judgement and condemnation that I was sure I deserved but wasn't ready to face. However, I soon ran out of breath and in my vision, my heavenly Father caught up with me.

As He did, I felt myself enveloped in love. It was the most wonderful feeling – warm and comforting and uplifting. However despite this, at the same time I was feeling totally unworthy, so aware of everything I had done wrong in my life, and here I was in the presence of the Holy One. I wanted to shrivel up and disappear and could totally understand Isaiah's despair when he cried out, "Woe to me! I am ruined! For I am a man of unclean lips, and I live among a people of unclean lips, and my eyes have seen the King, the Lord Almighty" (Isaiah 6:5).

I was so overwhelmed I couldn't stand upright and lay flat on the ground, face first. Yet my heavenly Father gently stood me to my feet. He embraced me and then said these special words to me: "I am love. You are my special daughter. You don't need to feel worthy; you just are."

As He said those words and I experienced His awesome love, I felt all condemnation falling from me and an incredible acceptance of who I was, despite all my failings in the past. I felt validated and whole. Even better, I felt the wonderful peace that only God can provide, that is beyond all understanding.

I learned from this encounter that our heavenly Father wants to have an intimate loving relationship with us. I believe the most powerful illustration of this is the story in the Bible of the father who greeted his prodigal son, running to him, throwing his arms around him and kissing him.

He did this for me too. In another amazing vision, my heavenly Father ran towards me with arms outstretched. Again, I was so overawed I just wanted to prostrate myself. At least this time I didn't try to run away! Again my heavenly Father gently lifted me to my feet. Then He put a ring on my finger and gave me sandals for my feet. My vision ended with Him telling me He was going to prepare a banquet for me.

I often get visions in which I encounter my heavenly Father. However, in most of these visions, my heavenly Father is glorious, sitting on His throne, the one described in Isaiah 6 and Revelation 4. It is an incredible sight and I am always overwhelmed with awe when I see Him. I don't see His face but I get the most incredible sense of His majesty.

In most of these visions, I am a little girl about five years old just wanting to be with her Dad. He lets me sit on His lap, where I always feel safe and secure no matter what is going on in my life. I once asked Him why I was the only one on His lap and He said, "I know how you love to be one-on-one!" However at the same time I asked if He had a message for others and He said He is waiting to show you His love.

The Father's Love

Lord, you're so kind and tenderhearted
    and so patient with people who fail you!
    Your love is like a flooding river
    overflowing its banks with kindness.

Higher than the highest heavens –
    that's how high your tender mercy extends!
    Greater than the grandeur of heaven above
    is the greatness of your loyal love, towering over all
    who fear you and bow down before you!
                      (Psalm 103:8,11 TPT)

Chapter 3
THE TRINITY

Christians believe God is one God but three persons (commonly referred to as the Trinity). They are:

- Our heavenly Father,
- His Son our Lord Jesus Christ; and
- The Holy Spirit.

All three members of the Trinity are referred to in the description of the stoning of Stephen in Acts 7:55-56:

> But Stephen, full of the Holy Spirit, looked up to heaven and saw the glory of God, and Jesus standing at the right hand of God. "Look," he said, "I see heaven open and the Son of Man standing at the right hand of God."

The glory of God is referring to our heavenly Father, Jesus is in heaven standing by our Father and the Holy Spirit is on earth empowering Stephen.

In the Lord's Prayer, we are told our Father is in heaven, which is why I refer to Him as our heavenly Father.

The Bible tells us that our heavenly Father is just like Jesus! Hebrews 1:3 says: "The Son is the radiance of God's glory and the exact representation of His being, sustaining all things by His powerful word."

We know what Jesus is like because of the detailed accounts in the Bible.

Our heavenly Father and Jesus are currently both in heaven. However, the Holy Spirit is here on earth with us. He is the spirit of the Father and the spirit of Jesus.

I have been blessed to encounter the Holy Spirit in various visions. He has appeared to me in different forms, but the most common is that of like swooshing, glittering dust with electricity flashing through it. As He swooshes around me I can feel His presence.

Other times, He has appeared as a man in His early thirties.

Sometimes I hear His words (as an internal impression, not an external voice) and I know He is present, but I cannot see Him.

In one wonderful vision, I encountered all three members of the Trinity. This is what I wrote in my journal at the time:

> Thank you so much that I could meet you – the Trinity – in the throne room – Jesus, your beautiful eyes of love; dear Father – your majesty, and dear Holy Spirit – a beautiful young man. And you lifted me up by removing the condemnation I was feeling. You raised me up and I felt your love and was reassured of your guidance and support, and I felt safe.
>
> And yet, Lord, I scarce can take it in that you, the creator of the universe, have a loving relationship with me, and I understand that it is through your healing love that I can reach out in love.

Thank you is not enough, Lord, but I thank you. Thank you that you said the battle is yours. I can rest in you now and let go and just be focused on being guided by you.

Chapter 4
MY STORY

I am one of those people who is always asking questions. Two of my major questions as a teenager were, "What is the meaning of life?" and "What happens when you die?"

I was absolutely terrified of dying and I wanted to be reassured that there was life after death. I wasn't brought up in a Christian family, so my search for answers led me to studying New Age books and beliefs, and different cults as well as Christianity.

Due to various encounters with Christians, when I was in my thirties I finally accepted that Christianity was the one theology that could best answer my questions.

By then I was going through an acrimonious divorce, had a young daughter and a high-profile job in a major Australian accounting firm. I was (and still am) a lawyer who specialises in taxation law. I had three university degrees and yet had not until then learnt about God's love for me.

After reading various books and debates on the issue, I finally could not refute (and therefore accepted) that Jesus had died on a cross and was resurrected after three days. I believed I was a Christian because I believed in Christ and His resurrection. However, I still didn't know God's love.

It wasn't until I was 39 that I was challenged on whether I truly was a Christian – one, who in the words of the Bible (Ephesians

4:22-24) has "put off the old self, which is being corrupted by its deceitful desires, made new the attitude of my mind, and put on the new self, created to be like God in true righteousness and holiness."

After about six months of constant challenge, I woke up one morning and finally grasped the enormity of Jesus willingly dying on the cross for me. Being willing to die for someone (and actually doing it) is an incredible act of love.

At the same time I realised I had done nothing to deserve that incredible sacrifice and in fact had done acts which deserved the opposite of love.

That realisation made me feel totally unworthy and yet incredibly grateful at the same time. That morning I accepted Jesus in my heart as well as my mind. My new comprehension of His love for me made me want to love Him back in every way I could. I was now willing to say the words Jesus said in the Garden of Gethsemane, "Not my will but yours be done" (Luke 22:42).

That realisation also led to a huge learning curve. I felt God was constantly highlighting areas of my life that needed to change.

I started reading the Bible – His Word. When I read the Old Testament I began to really understand the Father's heart for His people and also how hurt He was when they complained and disobeyed Him and started to worship other gods.

Then I started reading daily devotionals and they gave me more of an insight into the Bible. However, it was when I started to keep a gratitude journal that I began to hear from God. I would list all the things I was grateful for in the day (or week) and then I would ask God to speak to me, often asking for guidance in a certain area. I would write down the words I received and it was obvious they were not my words.

For example, one day I received the following:

> To my people I will bring peace.
> They will rise up under my anointing.
> I am your Lord, the anointed One
> Listen to my words and respond to them.
> I will raise you up to greater heights.
> And I will nurture you under my wings.
>
> Come to me you who are heavily laden.
> My yoke is light.
> I will bear your burdens for you.
> In return I give you my peace, my joy.
> Come to me.

At the same time I started the journal, I deliberately set aside time to focus on God. This was usually when I woke up in the morning and was still lying in bed. I asked Him questions and usually heard from Him. This is when the visions started. My visions are like dreams, except that I am wide awake when I receive them.

A few years after my divorce, God brought a lovely Christian man (Graham) into my life and we married more than 20 years ago.

I now know that the meaning of life is to worship God, to love and serve Him and to enjoy the wonderful things He has done and does for me.

God has taught me so much and now is guiding me in teaching others. He gives me special words of encouragement for people I pray over and I have seen many healings. A wonderful thing is that I have lost my fear of death. Every day I wake up knowing that God loves me, and no matter what happens to me here on earth, I can look forward to a glorious future with Him forever.

I can say from personal experience that knowing God's love and accepting it can radically transform your life.

God has made it clear to me that He wants everyone to know His love. He told me to write this book. He also gave me the vision I describe below that illustrates He wants you to have a relationship with Him.

I received the vision one morning at church when the worship music was playing. In the vision I was in heaven with thousands of others worshipping God. I could see my heavenly Father on the throne. Despite the thousands there, He looked directly at me and spoke to me. This of course made me feel very significant and special. However at the same time, I was wondering why He would do that for me – single me out like that. I asked, "Why me?"

His response was, "Those who seek me I will respond to and make myself known."

I checked with His Word and received these confirmations. Proverbs 8:17 says: "I love those who love me, and those who seek me find me."

Jeremiah 29:13 says: "You will seek me and find me when you seek me with all your heart."

I am not unique in receiving visions and hearing from God. God wants a relationship with you and He wants to communicate with you. In fact, He is already doing it now through this book!

Chapter 5
GOD'S LOVE COVENANT

Things were going wrong in my life and I just wanted to talk to Jesus about them. In a vision, I walked up some stairs and saw Jesus on my right. However, in front of me I could see a path lined on both sides with angels blowing long trumpets.

Suddenly, without warning, I was transformed. I was a beautiful bride dressed in a white wedding gown with a train and a veil.

Jesus then took my arm and we walked up the path together to the Father's throne where Jesus presented me as His bride. (Such a special vision. Thank you, Lord). Of course, when the vision ended the things that were going wrong in my life no longer had any impact on me. This is because I had been so impacted by the love of Jesus lavished on me.

Jesus loves us so much! So does our heavenly Father. John 3:16 tells us our heavenly Father loves us so much He gave His one and only Son (Jesus), so that whoever believes in Him shall not perish but have eternal life.

Our heavenly Father and His Son, our Lord Jesus Christ, covenanted that Jesus would give His life so that those who put their faith in Jesus and accepted Him as Lord and Saviour (I refer to these people as 'believers') would have eternal life, be forgiven all their sins and be made perfectly right with their heavenly Father and acceptable to Him so that they could approach Him.[1]

Our heavenly Father loves us so much that He gave His only Son to suffer in order for that to happen, and Jesus loves us so much that He was willing to go along with it. I call this God's love covenant.

Have you ever wondered "Why?" – I have.

My understanding is that we first have to realise that God, the creator of the universe, is all about relationship. He wants loving relationship with us (1 John 3:1; Mark 12:30).

God had a personal relationship with Adam and Eve. The Bible tells us He walked with them in the Garden of Eden. However, He gave Adam and Eve free choice so that they could freely choose whether to respond or not to His love. If God hadn't given them free choice, they would have been little more than puppets.

Unfortunately Adam and Eve chose to eat from the forbidden tree – something they were expressly told not to do. As a result of their disobedience, sin was introduced into the world and death and spiritual separation from God was the result. Romans 5:12 (TPT) says:

> When Adam sinned, the entire world was affected. Sin entered human experience, and death was the result. And so death followed this sin, casting its shadow over all humanity, because all have sinned.

Because we are all Adam's descendants, his sin has passed down

---

1. Ephesians 3:12 "In him (Jesus) and through faith in him we may approach God with freedom and confidence."

the line to us and we are all born sinners. Sinners have no right to approach our perfect, holy God. Not being able to approach Him is a huge barrier to relationship.

However, God knew this would happen and He loves us, so He provided a way for us to approach Him and once again be in relationship with Him – God's love covenant. What is amazing is that this was part of His plan before the creation of the world (see 1 Peter 1:18-20 if you don't believe me!).

A covenant is like a contract. At law, there needs to be consideration to make a contract enforceable. Jesus' blood, shed when He was crucified on the cross, was the consideration for this covenant. We know this because Jesus said: "This cup is the new covenant in my blood, which is poured out for you" (Luke 22:20).

The love covenant is also referred to as the new covenant of grace because it is a gift from God.

"Grace" has been described as: **God's Riches At Christ's Expense.** This is because it is a gift only made possible by the sacrifice Jesus made for us.

The new covenant of grace replaced the old covenant of law that God had made with the people of Israel when He led them out of Egypt. The old covenant required the people of Israel to perfectly obey the Ten Commandments and associated laws. Of course this was humanly impossible and the whole idea of the old covenant was to make the Israelites realise they could never obey the commandments without God's help.

By dying on the cross, Jesus enabled the new covenant of grace to come into effect[2] and replace the old covenant of law.

---

2. Hebrews 9:16-17 (MSG) "Like a will that takes effect when someone dies, the new covenant was put into action at Jesus' death. His

WHAT IS THE NEW COVENANT OF GRACE?

The new covenant of grace is detailed in Hebrews 8:10-13:

> This is the covenant I will establish with the people of
> Israel
> after that time, declares the Lord.
> I will put my laws in their minds
> and write them on their hearts.
> I will be their God,
> and they will be my people.
> No longer will they teach their neighbour,
> or say to one another, "Know the Lord,"
> because they will all know me,
> from the least of them to the greatest.
> For I will forgive their wickedness
> and will remember their sins no more.
> By calling this covenant "new," He has made the first one
> obsolete; and what is obsolete and outdated will soon
> disappear.

This covenant is for believers because we are grafted in as children of Abraham (the people of Israel referred to above). See Galatians 3:7-8.

Believers don't have to worry about keeping a whole series of laws the way the people of Israel were required to under the old

---

death marked the transition from the old plan to the new one, cancelling the old obligations and accompanying sins, and summoning the heirs to receive the eternal inheritance that was promised them. He brought together God and his people in this new way."

covenant. In fact, Paul warned strongly against returning to the law.[3] In Galatians 3:1-5, Paul said:

> You foolish Galatians! Who has bewitched you? Before your very eyes Jesus Christ was clearly portrayed as crucified. I would like to learn just one thing from you: Did you receive the Spirit by the works of the law, or by believing what you heard? Are you so foolish? After beginning by means of the Spirit, are you now trying to finish by means of the flesh? Have you experienced so much in vain – if it really was in vain? So again I ask, does God give you his Spirit and work miracles among you by the works of the law, or by your believing what you heard?

Grace is about being guided by God, not struggling to do the right thing in our own strength.

You (a believer) will know God's will because it will be on your mind and written on your heart. If God wants you to do something, He will make it clear to you and then empower you to do it (like me writing this book!).

Believers can let go and let God! You can never meet God's perfect standards in your own strength, so why beat yourself up about it? Instead, trust God to gently guide you in every situation.

---

3. In fact, Paul went so far as to say in Galatians 3:10-11, "For all who rely on the works of the law are under a curse, as it is written: 'Cursed is everyone who does not continue to do everything written in the Book of the Law.' Clearly no one who relies on the law is justified before God, because 'the righteous will live by faith.'"

You will know when He is guiding you because the result will be His fruit – love, joy, peace, forbearance, kindness, goodness, faithfulness, gentleness and self-control.

Note that under the covenant of grace, God also says that He will remember our sins no more. Our sins, past present and future, are forgiven forever because of the great sacrifice Jesus made.

If you are not yet a believer and you would like to be, I recommend you pray the prayer below and approach a Bible-based church that will guide you and support you.

> Dear Lord Jesus, I know that I am a sinner, and I ask for your forgiveness. I believe you died for my sins and rose from the dead. I turn from my sins and invite you to come into my heart and life. I want to trust and follow you as my Lord and Saviour. Amen.

Chapter 6
GOD MAKES US A NEW CREATION

I was woken up one morning by the Holy Spirit saying, "I am going to make everything new – Revelation 21:5. Read this a thousand times."

Those words led me to a study of the Bible to find all the references to 'new' in it. One that stood out was that as a result of the new covenant of grace (God's love covenant I referred to in the previous chapter), when we accept Jesus as our Lord and Saviour (our salvation), we automatically become new creations.

2 Corinthians 5:17 states that if anyone is in Christ, the new creation has come.

Ephesians 2:13 (TPT) says:

> *Look at you now! Everything is new!* Although you were once distant and far away from God, now you have been brought delightfully close to Him through the sacred blood of Jesus – you have actually been united to Christ!

I have already mentioned that according to the Bible, we are all Adam's descendants. We are all physically born into the family of Adam with the unfortunate consequence that we are all born sinners with spirits disconnected from God.

Because of God's great love for us, at salvation, our spirit becomes connected to God and we are spiritually born into the family of God.[4]

When you become a believer, you become a child of God who is 'in Christ', a new creation and a member of God's family. Not only that, but at the same time the Holy Spirit comes to reside within you.

1 John 4:15 says that if anyone acknowledges that Jesus is the Son of God, God lives in them and they in God.

Not only are we in Christ when we accept Jesus as our Lord and Saviour, He is also in us through His Holy Spirit. Paul said in Colossians 1:26-27 that this is:

> ... the mystery that has been kept hidden for ages and generations but is now disclosed to the Lord's people. To them God has chosen to make known among the Gentiles the glorious riches of this mystery, which is Christ in you, the hope of glory.

This means that God Himself resides within our bodies through the Holy Spirit!

God gave me this message: "I am the fullness of God in you – the new wineskin because you are a new creation!"

I find it amazing that the same Holy Spirit who was present at the creation of the world now resides within our bodies as a result of our salvation. The same power that raised Jesus from

---

4. John 1:12-13 "Yet to all who did receive him, to those who believed in his name, he gave the right to become children of God – children born not of natural descent, nor of human decision or a husband's will, but born of God."

the dead lives in us! In fact, believers are expressly instructed to be aware that their bodies are temples of the Holy Spirit, who is in them.

It is the Holy Spirit who empowers believers. He is the one who performs miracles; we are His vehicles. 2 Corinthians 4:7 states: "But we have this treasure in jars of clay to show that this all-surpassing power is from God and not from us."

Chapter 7
GOD GIVES US GIFTS

I had a vision in church where I looked up and it seemed like there were hundreds and hundreds of gifts hanging from the ceiling. They were there for the congregation. All they had to do was ask for them. There were gifts of wisdom, peace, discernment and joy as well as others.

I have discovered there are so many gifts that God lavishes on us when we become believers. Of course the greatest present of all is His presence!

I want to highlight the gifts I have listed below that are given to believers at their salvation:

- They become God's children
- God sees them as perfect
- God does not condemn them
- God forgives them all their sins forever
- They have eternal life.

Remember, these are all gifts – none of them are earned.

WE (BELIEVERS) BECOME GOD'S CHILDREN
God tells us that we are His beloved children. We are His family. It is a relationship of love as God is love. We are fully

accepted just as we are (with all our faults and baggage!) and totally loved.

Paul expressed this beautifully in Romans 8:15-16 (TPT):

> And you did not receive the "spirit of religious duty," leading you back into the fear *of never being good enough*. But you have received the "Spirit of full acceptance," enfolding you into the family of God. And you will never feel orphaned, for as He rises up within us, our spirits join Him in saying the words of tender affection, "Beloved Father!"
>
> For the Holy Spirit makes God's fatherhood real to us as He whispers into our innermost being, "You are God's beloved child!"

In an earlier chapter, I told you about the vision when Jesus rescued me from drowning and told me how He loved me so much He died for me.

Receiving that vision changed my life. It taught me that my significance in God's eyes is all that matters.

As believers, we are significant in God's eyes because we are who God says we are – deeply loved children of the glorious Creator of the Universe.

You are a beloved child of God. This is your new identity statement. Never compare yourself with others because it is not what others think of you or what the world says about you that matters. God's opinion of you is the only one that matters. My heavenly Father has assured me: "You are royalty. You are mine. I am the King and you are my precious daughter."

Another time, He said: "You are original. Everyone is. You

are all masterpieces, not one the same as the other. Ponder on this."

When we identify with our new identity in Christ, we learn to be empowered by the Holy Spirit. 1 John 5:4-5 (TPT) says:

> *You see*, every child of God overcomes the world, for our faith is the victorious power that triumphs over the world. So who are the world conquerors, *defeating its power*? Those who believe that Jesus is the Son of God.

The evil one doesn't want this, so be prepared for attacks on your identity. He even attacked Jesus when He was in the wilderness. Remember, God's opinion of you is the only one that matters. The Holy Spirit gave me these words for you: "When I look in the mirror, what do I see? A person of beauty looking back at me."

OUR HEAVENLY FATHER SEES US AS PERFECT

I can say this because the Bible tells us that when we become new creations, we receive the righteousness of God, which is God's perfect standard (2 Corinthians 5:21). The 'righteousness of God' is the standard necessary to approach our heavenly Father who is perfect and holy. He cannot allow sin to come near Him.

Only Jesus has ever met this perfect standard.

Paul tells us in Romans 5:1-2 that our faith in Jesus transfers God's righteousness to us. What this means is that, in the eyes of God, we are now seen as perfect. Our heavenly Father sees us as holy, without blemish and free from accusation (Colossians 1:22-23). This is despite the fact that we are obviously not perfect. It is because of what Jesus did in allowing Himself to be crucified for us.

In a wonderful vision I was clothed in the robe of righteousness by Jesus knowing that I had done nothing to deserve it – it was all Jesus's doing. However, not only that, Jesus then crowned me with His crown of righteousness. As you can imagine, I was totally overwhelmed. Also, I didn't know it then but found out later that 2 Timothy 4:8 states: "Now there is in store for me the crown of righteousness, which the Lord, the righteous Judge, will award to me on that day – and not only to me, but also to all who have longed for His appearing."

We only receive the righteousness of God by faith in Jesus Christ. It is easy for us as it is a free gift. However, it cost our heavenly Father dearly. He paid for it with the blood of His only Son, Jesus Christ.[5]

Sometimes we think that by doing good works, God will see us as righteous. Certainly, doing good works is commendable and the Bible urges us to do them. However, they can never meet God's perfect standard. Isaiah 64:6 tells us that all our righteous acts are like filthy rags. We don't have the power to be righteous on our own.

This was illustrated to me in another vision. I was in a muddy pit and filthy. I couldn't get out and was crying out to God for help. Then Jesus appeared at the top of the pit and let down a rope of light. My fingers seemed to attach to it and I felt myself being lifted up and pulled out of the pit. When I reached the top, Jesus embraced me, then led me under a waterfall where all the filth washed away. Then He dressed me in a beautiful white robe of righteousness.

---

5. Galatians 2:21 "I do not set aside the grace of God, for if righteousness could be gained through the law (our works), Christ died for nothing!"

It is Christ's righteousness that is imputed to us and never our own righteousness. Therefore we also need to be careful of becoming 'self-righteous'. Unfortunately this was a characteristic of the Pharisees and Jesus was quite scathing in His comments about them!

GOD DOES NOT CONDEMN US

In Romans 8:1 is the wonderful statement that there is now no condemnation for those who are in Christ Jesus. I love this statement by Paul – it is so freeing. It is also supported by John 3:16-17:

> For God so loved the world that He gave His one and only Son, that whoever believes in Him shall not perish but have eternal life. For God did not send His Son into the world to condemn the world, but to save the world through Him.

Jesus came not to condemn the world, but to save it. He illustrated how God does not condemn sinners when He spoke to the woman who was caught in adultery. He did not condemn her. Instead He told her to go and leave her life of sin.

Paul struggled with the fact that, despite being a Christian, he still committed sins. He said in Romans 7:15: "I do not understand what I do. For what I want to do I do not do, but what I hate I do."

That is why he delighted in the fact there is no condemnation for those in Christ Jesus.

God views believers as cleansed of all guilt, shame and condemnation because they are the righteousness of God in

Christ Jesus. Yet most of us experience condemnation, whether it is self-condemnation or comes from others. I am sure most of us would agree that we are often our own worst critics.

Condemnation drags us down. It creates shame and guilt. It points out what a failure we are; that we have made a terrible mess of things ... the list goes on.

However, we need to know that condemnation (including self-condemnation) comes from the evil one. John says in Revelation 12:10 that Satan is our accuser. He is the one who wants to destroy us by tearing us down.

If we think condemnation comes from God, the shame and guilt will make us think that God is unhappy with us and we will doubt His love for us. That is why it is so important to take hold of this truth – there is no condemnation for those who are in Christ Jesus.

God confirmed this in a vision a few years ago. I was feeling particularly condemned for a number of reasons. I spoke to my Lord about it, handing the condemnation to Him and thanking Him that I could ask Him for guidance, and these are the words I received: "You are right; the condemnation does not come from me. Use your authority to bind it and then to release the Spirit of love and peace."

Another time I received these words: "Always remain in my love, shake off condemnation and repent quickly of any offence given or taken. I am always with you and I love you always."

The Holy Spirit will never condemn us. He is the Spirit of Jesus and of our heavenly Father. However, He will gently convict in love. Conviction is quite different to condemnation. It will not tear us down the way condemnation does. Instead, the conviction of the Holy Spirit will comfort us and lift us up and guide us in the way to go. Jesus called the Holy Spirit our comforter. He will reassure us of God's love for us and restore us.

Some time ago I was feeling down during a church service. I didn't feel able to engage at all. During the worship time, I sat down and asked God for help. I received the following vision which I journalled as follows:

> I could see Jesus and my heavenly Father sitting down with a bright light all around them in the far distance. Between me and them were thousands of people all worshipping. I was on the absolute outer limit feeling totally out of it.
>
> Then the Holy Spirit appeared to me and asked me what was wrong and I told Him. He then transported me so that suddenly there I was with Jesus, the heavenly Father and the Holy Spirit and they all embraced me. The love I felt was indescribable.

When we realise and understand that there is therefore now no condemnation in Christ, we can stop condemning ourselves.

When self-condemnation stops, then condemnation of others will stop as well. I have observed this about myself. When I was attacked by a spirit of self-condemnation, I noticed that I was quite critical in my words in talking about others and it came from this spirit because I was so critical about myself. I needed to be loving and non-critical of myself first so that I could then relate that way to others.

Jesus told us to love our neighbour as ourselves (Mark 12:31). This means we need to love ourselves first so that we can then love others.

GOD FORGIVES US ALL OUR SINS FOREVER

God has forgiven us all our sins.[6] All the sins we have committed in the past and will commit in the future are forgiven. How can that be?

It is because of the love covenant sealed with the blood of Jesus. Jesus sacrificed for our sins once and for all when He allowed himself to be the sin offering on the cross – the ultimate final sacrifice (Hebrews 7:27).

Jesus Himself said, "It is finished." His work is complete and we are forgiven for all time. This means we are justified – God sees us 'just as if' we have never sinned.

The Message version of Hebrews 10:14 is a wonderful summary of what Jesus did for us on the cross. It states: "It was a perfect sacrifice by a perfect person to perfect some very imperfect people!" Through Jesus Christ, we have had our sins forgiven and we have been set free from the power of sin.

When we accept Jesus as our Lord and Saviour, we become a new creation. We are miraculously changed and we are no longer slaves to sin (Romans 6:3-7, 14). When we do sin, we can quickly respond to the loving conviction of the Holy Spirit and become empowered by Him to overcome the sin.

However, knowing that we have forgiveness from our sins is not a licence to go out and sin. Paul was very emphatic about this in his letter to the Romans. We need to know that even when we put our faith in Jesus, and despite what Jesus has done for us, we will still be tempted to sin.

---

6. God said in Jeremiah 31:34, repeated in Hebrews 8:12, "… I will forgive their wickedness and will remember their sins *no more*." No more means never, ever!

However, the temptation can be overcome and we do this by giving it to God. If we try to do it in our own strength, we will struggle. When something goes wrong, for example, if you find it very hard to forgive someone, the best thing to do is hand it to God. Whatever your issue, I recommend the following prayer:

Dear heavenly Father, I am sorry. Thank you that I am forgiven and you do not condemn me. Thank you for your everlasting love. Thank you that I can hand this issue to you for resolution (fill in the details). In the name of Jesus. Amen.

He will enable us to overcome (Philippians 2:13). Not only that, when we hand over our issues with thanksgiving, Philippians 4:6-7 tells us that God will actually then reward us by giving us His perfect peace.

WE HAVE ETERNAL LIFE
God so loved the world that He gave His one and only Son, that whoever believes in Him shall not perish but have eternal life (John 3:16). Eternal life means life with no end.

It is hard to contemplate eternity. I don't think our human brains have the capacity to completely grasp what it means. It is also incredible to realise that eternity starts as soon as we give our life to Jesus. For me, it is wonderful to know that I will be with my God, who is love, forever.

CHAPTER 8
GOD'S PLANS FOR US

Did you know that before you were born, God had made wonderful plans for you which are all written in His book? Also that He created you to reflect His glory (Isaiah 43:7)?

This was a bit of a revelation for me. However it clearly states in Psalm 139:16: "Your eyes saw my unformed body; all the days ordained for me were written in your book before one of them came to be."

It is incredible to realise that God has a plan for each one of us that was recorded before we were even born.

If we were created to reflect His glory, how do we do that?

Well, when you become a believer, the glory of God comes to reside within you. Then the Bible tells us that when we contemplate His glory, we become transformed into His image. 2 Corinthians 3:18 states:

> And we all, who with unveiled faces contemplate the Lord's glory, are being transformed into His image with ever-increasing glory, which comes from the Lord, who is the Spirit.

In a vision, I was with Jesus and suddenly He grew huge in stature in front of me. I was tiny in comparison. I only reached up to the top of His ankles! Then Jesus reached down and put His hands under my shoulders and I grew up to His height. Jesus said to me, "The greater you see me, the greater you will magnify me in the world."

By deliberately stepping into God's plans for our life, we reflect His glory.

How do we know what these plans are? The best way to find out is to ask God. He says in Psalm 32:8-9 (TPT):

> I will stay close to you,
> instructing and guiding you along the pathway for your life.
> I will advise you along the way
> and lead you forth with my eyes as your guide.
> So don't make it difficult; don't be stubborn
> when I take you where you've not been before.
> Don't make me tug you and pull you along.
> Just come with me!

I asked God His plans for me and His response was that He is giving me a message (i.e. the contents of this book) that I am to share with the world.

If you don't get an answer, then the next best way to find out is to focus on your heart desires. Because God created us, our longings and passions are clues to His plans for us here on earth.

The talents He has given us are also a guide to His plans for us. He has given each one of us different talents. Some may love singing, dancing, painting, writing ... I love teaching. One day I journaled the following: "You pulled me out of the miry clay and set me free to go and play!"

It seems that what we love doing is part of God's plans for us.

Also, as believers, we need to realise that each one of us becomes part of the body of Christ with a different part to play (1 Corinthians 12:27). Knowing where we fit in will also be a guide for us. For me, that is to teach. You may find yourself called in a different area, for example, to pastor.

We need to be aware, though, that Satan will do anything to stop us realising God's plans for our lives and we live in a world which is currently under Satan's control.[7] Sometimes he will oppose those plans by burdening us with resentments or worries that distract us. Even as I was writing this chapter, I received disturbing news which made me hesitate to go on further until I realised what was going on.

Don't let Satan tell you that your time is past, that you are too old, stupid, unqualified – whatever it is that he throws at you to try to thwart God's plans for your life. It is all lies, and Jesus told us that the evil one is the master of lies (John 8:44).

Write down the desires God has put in your heart. Claim them and visualise them coming to life. Start focusing on the positive and not the negative.

What if you have received a promise from God and you are waiting to see it fulfilled? Well, I have written a chapter on perseverance later on. However, let me encourage you to hang in there. God taught me about perseverance several years ago and then the next topics were 'patience' and 'His strength' – I am sure those topics were linked for a reason.

I found this blog, written by Lana Vawser (an Australian prophet), incredibly encouraging:[8]

---

7. 1 John 5:19 "We know that we are children of God, and that the whole world is under the control of the evil one."
8. Lana Vawser Ministries, prophetic words, 5 September 2017.

I heard the Lord say today, "I AM SHIFTING THE 'WHAT IFS'." I saw many of God's people wrestling with 'what ifs' and the things I noticed about the 'what ifs' many were wrestling with, were they were all negative. "What if this happens?" "What if that happens?"

Fear whispering and shouting the "what ifs" regarding the future, people and situations that were bringing unrest, anxiety and fear. I then heard the Lord make a decree and His decree was: "WHAT IF!!!" But HIS "what if" was full of hope, expectancy, joy, breakthrough and miracles.

... He's whispering, "What if this is the prayer that will bring your breakthrough?" "What if that step of faith and obedience will see you move into joy like you have never seen or experienced?" "What if the enemy is attempting to derail you and attack you because of the large breakthrough of destiny upon you?" "What if this is the day and season of your greatest breakthrough?"

It is very reassuring to know that anything God calls us to do He will empower us to do. 1 Peter 4:11 says: "... If anyone serves, they should do so with the strength God provides, so that in all things God may be praised through Jesus Christ."

We are also told in 2 Peter 1:3: "His divine power has given us everything we need for a godly life through our knowledge of Him who called us by His own glory and goodness."

We will know when we are operating in God's strength because that is when we see the fruit of the Holy Spirit – love, joy, peace, forbearance, kindness, goodness, faithfulness, gentleness and self-control.

It means no more striving and attempting to do things in our own strength. When we feel drained by our Christian endeavours, that is often a sure sign we are striving.

Chapter 9
RESTING IN THE VICTORY OF CHRIST JESUS

1 Chronicles 29:11 (KJV):

> Yours, O Lord, is the greatness, the power, and the glory, the victory and the majesty; for all that is in heaven and in earth is yours; yours is the kingdom, O Lord, and you are exalted as head over all.

This is how Jesus told me it works: "OK, my darling, this is how it is. I love you. You love me. I love the world. You love me so you will love the world too with my love. Don't beat yourself up about your inadequacies. They are irrelevant. It is all about *my* love, *my* power and *my* victory – which you get to participate in because you are now part of me. Rejoice and dance. You know my love. That is all that matters. All I want you to do is share your experiences of my love. That's all."

Jesus has already won the battle against Satan and made a public spectacle of him and his powers and authorities. Jesus won the victory and we win it too through our faith in Jesus Christ (1 Corinthians 15:57). Our victory is a grace gift from God.

The fact that Jesus has defeated death, Satan and the power of sin does not mean that we have protection from attacks here on earth. We will still face trials as our world is currently under the power of the devil (1 John 5:19) and he is determined to destroy us while he has the chance. He will use any means to attack our health, marriage, children, finances, relationships … and he will try to destroy our faith. He will attempt to set up strongholds in our lives, for example, strongholds of anger, fear and pride.

However, we have the victory. We *don't* access it by rebuking Satan because he will just increase his attacks and make our situation worse. We have the victory through Christ. The battles aren't ours; they are God's (1 Samuel 17:47). No matter what trials you are facing, God has already conquered them! We can rest in His victory by believing that and acting accordingly.

We know that God has it under control, so we thank Him that He does and for His love. It won't matter if you don't instantly see the healing that you are praying for or the salvation of a loved one as you can rest in the assurance that God has already won the battle and you will see the victory in His perfect timing.

This was illustrated to me in a vision I received after a big week of feeling drained by people's needs and overwhelmed with my work commitments. I was definitely under attack and at the end of the week, I sought God's help (memo to self – don't wait so long next time!).

In the vision I could see a black fighter jet, aiming for me and shooting missiles. I realised that Satan was trying to take me out. I put up my arm and saw there was a glowing white shield that protected me from the missiles and from the jet plane itself.

Then I realised it was no longer me who was holding the shield, it was Jesus and I was holding onto His legs – in height I only came up to His knees. He said to leave Him with the shield and to go spend time with my heavenly Father.

Next thing I knew, I was sitting on my heavenly Father's lap as a little girl feeling all safe and secure and loved. We both could see Jesus holding the shield and fending off the attacks.

My heavenly Father said, "See, Jesus is fighting your battles for you."

Another time, I was walking one morning speaking out loud to Jesus and asking Him questions. One was, "How do you do what you do?" His answer (not an audible voice, but a definite impression) was, "I am God."

When I commented that I would find it impossible, His response was, "You're not God!"

That made me chuckle. It also was a huge relief. I am not God, therefore I don't have to do the things He does. *He* will do it for me for He is with me wherever I go.

I have God's Spirit within me to do the work. I can relax, and literally apply the words in Philippians 4:6-7 which say, "Do not be anxious about *anything*, but in *every situation*, by prayer and petition, with thanksgiving, present your requests to God. And the peace of God, which transcends all understanding, will guard your hearts and your mind in Christ Jesus."

Every one of us has at least one worry that is a burden. *We have to take hold of the truth that Jesus wants us to hand ALL our worries and negative issues to Him.*

When our enemy is too big for us to handle there is only one thing to do – be totally dependent on God. The wonderful thing is that God wants us to be dependent on Him. That was an incredible revelation for me as I was brought up to be very independent.

God once said to me, "Look to me for your provision, not the world. I am your provider." Jesus specifically said:

Are you tired? Worn out? Burned out on religion? Come to me. Get away with me and you'll recover your life. I'll show you how to take a real rest. Walk with me and work with me – watch how I do it. Learn the unforced rhythms of grace. I won't lay anything heavy or ill-fitting on you. Keep company with me and you'll learn to live freely and lightly.

(Matthew 11:28-30 MSG)

I love the Message version of this passage as it so clearly tells us that we will learn to truly rest just by going to Jesus and walking and working with Him.

WHAT IS THIS REST REFERRED TO?

Peace, joy, hope, strength, stillness, tranquillity, contentment ... not worrying. It enables us to stop all our striving and let go of feelings of fear, guilt, shame, not quite measuring up, and so on.

Resting in Him involves handing any issues over to Him and trusting in Him that He will deal with them. It results in us letting go and letting God – completely trusting in His promises and that He has everything under control.

Can you imagine resting in peace and serenity and joy no matter what the circumstances?

You may be suffering from an addiction such as food, cigarettes, alcohol, drugs, computer games. No matter how hard you try, you can't let go. I personally have struggled in the past with addictions to computer games.

Self-discipline and willpower are *not* the way to overcome. *The secret is to hand the addiction over to God with gratitude that He will deal with it.* One way to pray is:

I give up, Lord. I cannot stop this in my own strength. I confess and repent of (name the addiction). I thank you Lord that I can hand it to you and I can depend on you to set me free. I praise you Lord. Amen.

This way there is no self-condemnation, just total reliance on the power of God. He will set you free. It may be immediate, it may take some time – His timing is always perfect. He may give you a strategy; He may not. However, in the interim, each time you light up a cigarette, play another computer game, and so on, say: "I cannot give this up Lord, but I know that you can and you will set me free."

One day you will find the cravings are gone. God will have set you free.

WE DO NEED TO TRUST

To rest in God, we need to have a relationship with Him and also trust that He is a good God and that He will keep His promises.

We have a relationship with God through spending time with Him. Remember that Jesus said to keep company with Him and we'll learn to live freely and lightly (Matthew 11:30 MSG).

As we grow in intimate relationship, we will grow in our understanding of His love for us and we will grow in our trust in Him and His promises. Relationship together with trust is really another name for faith.

You may wonder how a loving God could allow a loved one to suffer, or allow you to struggle financially. However, Proverbs 3:5 says: "Trust in the Lord with all your heart and lean not on your own understanding."

Therefore it is necessary that when we ask God to resolve an issue, we believe and act in the belief that He will.

Jesus is our perfect role model when it comes to trust. Remember that when the disciples were terrified of a storm and panicking, Jesus was asleep in the boat. When we completely trust God, it looks like Jesus peacefully resting in the back of the boat while a storm is raging.

God *is* all-powerful *and* He loves us. There is *no* point in not trusting Him as He is the only one who can be trusted.

There is always a reason for a storm but it is never because God doesn't love us. God's ways are not our ways. Job discovered this when he asked God why he had to suffer so much. God's response was not an apology. Instead, He said: "I will question you, and you shall answer me. Where were you when I laid the earth's foundation?" (Job 38:3-4).

Whenever I contemplate this passage, I feel the fear of God. He is the creator of the universe and yet out of His great love has provided a way for us to have relationship with Him and be part of His family. How dare we question Him?

In fact, when we do question Him we are effectively saying, "Why didn't you do it the way I wanted?" It is a form of pride because in doing so we are saying our ways are better than His.

My favourite Bible passage at times like these is Romans 8:28: "And we know that in all things God works for the good of those who love Him, who have been called according to His purpose."

Instead of questioning God, call out to Him for comfort and support and guidance. Rest in His love for you. Trust He has the victory. Let Him restore you and give you His supernatural peace.

When we rest in the Lord, we will have His peace. Storms will rage around us but we will be able to sleep through them. When we focus on what Jesus has done for us and trust Him with our issues, we will find the words of this wonderful chorus are true for us too:

> Turn your eyes upon Jesus
> Look full in His wonderful face.
> And the things of earth will grow strangely dim,
> In the light of His glory and grace.

I have reproduced two beautiful excerpts below from the Psalms on trusting God.
Psalm 37:3-9 (TPT):

> Keep trusting in the Lord and do what is right in his eyes.
> > Fix your heart on the promises of God and you will
> > be secure,
> > feasting on his faithfulness.
> Find your delight and true pleasure in Yahweh,
> > and he will give you what you desire the most.
> Give God the right to direct your life,
> > and as you trust him along the way
> > you'll find he pulled it off perfectly!
> He will appear as your righteousness,
> > as sure as the dawning of a new day.
> > He will manifest as your justice,
> > as sure and strong as the noonday sun.
> Quiet your heart in his presence
> > and wait patiently for Yahweh.
> > And don't think for a moment that the wicked in their
> > prosperity
> > are better off than you.

Stay away from anger and revenge.
>   Keep envy far from you, for it only leads you into lies.
> For one day the wicked will be destroyed,
>   but those who trust in the Lord
>   will inherit the land.

Psalm 56:9-13 (TPT):
> The very moment I call to you for a father's help
>   the tide of battle turns and my enemies flee.
>   This one thing I know: God is on my side!
> I trust in the Lord. And I praise him!
>   I trust in the Word of God. And I praise him!
> What harm could man do to me?
>   With God on my side I will not be afraid of what comes.
>   My heart overflows with praise to God and for his promises.
>   I will always trust in him.
> So I'm thanking you with all my heart,
>   with gratitude for all you've done.
>   I will do everything I've promised you, Lord.
> For you have saved my soul from death
>   and my feet from stumbling
>   so that I can walk before the Lord
>   bathed in his life-giving light.

WHAT IF WE STRUGGLE TO TRUST?

If you have had experiences in the past that are proving a real barrier to trusting in God, I strongly recommend receiving Christian counselling so that those barriers can be dealt with and removed. I personally have needed to do this to fully recover from some traumas I have experienced.

Chapter 10
UNITE AND FIGHT

A few years ago I received the following words from the Holy Spirit: "Body of Christ, unite and fight with the weapons of peace and love; signs and wonders."

I was intrigued by this message and started analysing it word by word. The first part was, "Body of Christ, unite and fight."

THE BODY OF CHRIST
The Body of Christ are those who accept Jesus as their Lord and Saviour (1 Corinthians 12:27).

WE ARE TO UNITE
Paul addressed this in Ephesians 4:1-6 when he said:

> As a prisoner for the Lord, then, I urge you to live a life worthy of the calling you have received. Be completely humble and gentle; be patient, bearing with one another in love. Make every effort to keep the unity of the Spirit through the bond of peace. There is one body and one Spirit, just as you were called to one hope when you were called; one Lord, one faith, one baptism; one God and Father of all, who is over all and through all and in all.

WE ARE TO FIGHT

I struggled to understand why we are to fight when Satan has already been defeated by Jesus. Jesus won the victory and we win it too through our faith in Him (1 Corinthians 15:57).

I finally understood that our fight is to prevent Satan having influence over us and others in any way that breaks the two great commandments:

- Love the Lord your God with all your heart, and with all your soul, and with all your mind; and
- Love your neighbour as yourself.

We do this by resting in Christ's victory (which I have already discussed); taking our thoughts captive (discussed below) and by wielding our spiritual weapons.

Paul explained in 2 Corinthians 10:3-5:

> For though we live in the world, we do not wage war as the world does. The weapons we fight with are not the weapons of the world. On the contrary, they have divine power to demolish strongholds. We demolish arguments and every pretension that sets itself up against the knowledge of God, and we take captive every thought to make it obedient to Christ.

The strongholds Paul refers to are those in our minds and in the minds of others. They are based on life experiences and the lies that we may believe as a result. They can wreak havoc in your life and they allow Satan to have influence over us without us even realising it.

For example, you may have been brought up by a very strict

and unloving father. This may have established a stronghold in your mind that your heavenly Father is the same as your earthly father and therefore not to be trusted. This is likely to prevent you from responding to His love.

These strongholds of the evil one need to be demolished so that we can know the truth about God's love for us and the truth can then set us free.

We demolish them by renewing our mind. This involves deliberately taking our thoughts captive so that our basic thinking patterns change. If our basic thinking patterns don't change, then our life won't either. The way we think rules our life.

Did you know that your thought life can actually make you sick? Dr Caroline Leaf, a neuroscientist who wrote the book *Who switched off my brain?* states that it has been proven that 75 to 95 percent of the illnesses that plague us today are a direct result of our thought life.

The average person has more than 30,000 thoughts a day. Through an uncontrolled thought life, we make ourselves sick! In fact, research shows that fear, all on its own, triggers more than 1,400 known physical and chemical responses.

Dr Leaf says the good news is that toxic thoughts, emotions and attitudes are controllable. We can control the incoming information before it wires into our brain – we have about 48 hours to do this. Neuroscience highlights the biblical principle that we must be responsible for our thought life, bringing every thought into captivity and renewing our minds.[9]

---

9. Romans 12:2 "Do not conform to the pattern of this world, but be transformed by the renewing of your mind. Then you will be able to test and approve what God's will is – his good, pleasing and

We need to grasp the fact that none of our negative thoughts come from God. Accepting they are not of God and then being committed to giving them to God and replacing them with His thoughts is the "taking your thoughts captive" process.

For example, if you have just had a fight with someone, your natural response will probably be one of anger and self-righteousness. However, God loves the person you have just fought with. He wants you to love him or her as well. I suggest you pray a prayer such as the following:

> Dear heavenly Father, I am sorry for fighting with (name of person). Thank you for your forgiveness. However, I am still very angry with him/her. I know that you love him/her. I lay my anger (and any other negative emotions) at the foot of the cross of Jesus. Please would you make your love for him/her now flow through me? Thank you. I say this in the name of Jesus. Amen.

I find that when I do this, I am switching my focus off myself and onto God. Most times, the effect of this prayer is that I am quickly able to recover from the hurt and anger.

Paul said, "Finally, brothers and sisters, whatever is true, whatever is noble, whatever is right, whatever is pure, whatever is lovely, whatever is admirable – if anything is excellent or praiseworthy – think about such things" (Philippians 4:8).

Therefore, the moment you think, for example, thoughts of fear or resentment, immediately turn to Jesus and ask for help

---

perfect will." 2 Corinthians 10:5 "…take captive every thought to make it obedient to Christ."

and guidance in the situation. Occupy your mind with thoughts of Jesus and His love for you and His victory over Satan.

By thinking correctly according to God's Word, we can actually change the structure of our brain to be what it should be. We may not be able to control the events and circumstances of our life, but we can control our reactions.

In other words, we are not helpless victims, but we do have a responsibility to take every thought captive to Christ, to repent, and to renew our minds. Our job is to analyse a thought before we decide either to accept or reject it. It is an exercise in awareness with incredible rewards.

Knowing our spiritual weapons will help us in this process. As I mentioned earlier, the words I received were: "Body of Christ, unite and fight with the weapons of peace and love, signs and wonders."

I had never thought of peace and love as being weapons. However, the more I researched, the more I realised that they are actually very potent weapons for advancing God's kingdom. As a result, I then started to research other weapons in our spiritual arsenal, a number of which I explore in later chapters. I start with the weapon of peace.

CHAPTER 11
THE WEAPON OF PEACE

Paul tells us in Romans 8:6 that the mind governed by the Holy Spirit is life and peace. Therefore, we access peace by allowing the Holy Spirit to govern our mind.

We allow our mind to be governed by the Holy Spirit by following the steps outlined in Philippians 4:6. There, Paul tells us to not be anxious about anything, but in every situation, by prayer and petition, with thanksgiving, to present our requests to God. When we do this, he says the peace of God, which transcends all understanding, will guard our hearts and our minds in Christ Jesus.

Straightaway, we can see that this peace of God is an effective weapon against fear and anxiety. It guards our hearts and minds from the attacks of the evil one.

We can also see that the steps outlined in Philippians 4:6 describe exactly the "taking every thought captive to Christ" process that we have just discussed.

We can be attacked with thoughts of fear and anxiety over a whole range of things, such as our children, our finances, our health, our future. However, these thoughts are all an attack from the evil one. They don't come from God. By being aware that we are under attack when we have these thoughts, we can then hand them over to God, thanking God that we can, and claiming His promise that His peace will dispel the fear.

For example, perhaps you are really anxious about a seminar you have to give the next day and you are tossing and turning in bed and unable to sleep. I suggest the following prayer:

Dear heavenly Father, I give you all my anxiety about the seminar. I want it to go well. Thank you that I can hand my fear and anxiety to you. Thank you for your love and support. I pray that your love will pour through me for the people at the seminar and that your love for me will pour through them. I say this in the name of Jesus. Amen.

You will know your mind is being governed by the Holy Spirit when you receive God's supernatural peace. It doesn't mean the circumstances have changed. What will change will be your reaction to the circumstances.

The answer is not the solution sought, but peace through loving relationship with God that enables you to go through the circumstances.

Jesus told His followers, "I have told you these things, so that in me you may have peace. In this world you will have trouble. But take heart! I have overcome the world" (John 16:33).

In a vision, when I was sitting beside Jesus looking down over the Sea of Galilee, Jesus told me the Sea represented the sea of life. He said it can be calm, but storms can also arise – especially when the devil is trying to stop us from reaching the other side. The good news is that we can also 'sleep through' the storms like Jesus did when He was here on earth (Mark 4:38), and we do this by accessing His peace.

Remember, we do this by allowing our mind to be governed

by the Holy Spirit. We are not victims of whatever thoughts come into our head. As I have mentioned, we can take our thoughts captive. When we don't do this we are vulnerable to Satan's attacks.

For example, one morning I awoke feeling very depressed. I went for a long walk and asked Jesus for help. On my walk, Jesus came to me in a vision and in that vision, we were both in a boat on the Sea of Galilee. It was very stormy on the sea and the waves were fierce. Jesus said I was in the middle of a storm and being assaulted with waves of resentment, bitterness and depression.

Jesus pointed out the shore to me and the blue sky above it that I could see from the boat. He told me I would make it to the shore and, in the meantime, to be reassured that He was there beside me in the boat.

Such a wonderful vision – so reassuring, and the depression went. When we know God's love and know 'He is in the boat with us', the assaults of the enemy can no longer impact us.

Yet it requires faith to hand anxieties and fears to God (and not take them back!). We can see this through Jesus' response to the disciples when they were scared in the boat with Him. He said, "Why are you so afraid? Do you still have no faith?" (Mark 4:40).

So many times I have prayed, received God's peace and then been tormented by the same thoughts a few hours later. However, I have found that the more I become aware of my negative thoughts and deliberately hand them to God, the more I experience His supernatural peace, and the less those thoughts will come back to torment me. When they do, I have found that the best thing to do is hand them over again and finally I stop taking them back. As a result, faith will increase and I am able to sing the words of this beautiful song sincerely:

It is Well with My Soul

When peace like a river attendeth my way,
When sorrows like sea billows roll
Whatever my lot, thou *hast taught me to say*
It is well, it is well, with my soul

It is well (it is well)
With my soul (with my soul)
It is well, it is well with my soul

Though Satan should buffet, though trials should come,
Let this blest assurance control,
That Christ has regarded my helpless estate,
And hath shed His own blood for my soul

It is well (it is well)
With my soul (with my soul)
It is well, it is well with my soul.

Did you know that peace is also a weapon against ill health? Proverbs 14:30 states: "A peaceful heart leads to a healthy body" (NLT).

Think about how you feel when you are fearful or stressed about something. Now contrast how you feel when you are at rest and peaceful. When was the last time someone asked how you were doing and your response included the word 'peaceful'? Wouldn't it be lovely if that was our normal response as opposed to "I am so busy" or "I am so stressed"?

Chapter 12
THE WEAPON OF LOVE

During worship in church, I went into a vision where I was sitting on my heavenly Father's lap and enjoying hugging Him and being hugged back. Then my heavenly Father put me on His knee and told me to look down.

When I did, I could see our planet Earth in darkness. My sight then zeroed in and I saw a stabbing in a street, and then I heard a gossip backstabbing. My heavenly Father asked me what I saw. My response was, "Brokenness because the people don't know your love."

He said, "Yes, and what is the greatest weapon that will overcome their brokenness?" I realised the answer and responded, "Your love." The greatest weapon Christians have against Satan is love. I can say this because through the power of His love, Jesus, while dying on the cross, was able to say, "Father, forgive them, for they do not know what they are doing."

CHARACTERISTICS OF LOVE

Love never fails. Love is patient, love is kind. It does not envy, it does not boast, it is not proud. It does not dishonour others, it is not self-seeking, it is not easily angered, it keeps no record of wrongs. Love does not delight in evil but rejoices with the truth.

Knowing God's Love

It always protects, always trusts, always hopes, and always perseveres (1 Corinthians 13:4-7).

Of course, because we know that God is love, this describes all His attributes!

When Jesus was asked the greatest commandment in the law, He said, "Love the Lord your God with all your heart and with all your soul and with all your mind. This is the first and greatest commandment. And the second is like it: 'Love your neighbour as yourself'" (Matthew 22:37-39).

Satan is opposed to this. He is the opposite of love and seeks to steal, kill and destroy. An example of this was how he sought to destroy the relationship Adam and Eve had with God.

Because we are in a spiritual battle, we need to be aware that the battle is not against people; it is for people. No matter how evil a person's actions can be, they are still loved by God, and their redemption is only a prayer away (Romans 10:13).

PERFECT LOVE CASTS OUT FEAR

In my early thirties, I was living in Sydney, Australia, and pregnant with my second child when I discovered that my husband was having an affair with a woman at his work. I miscarried the next day in the doctor's waiting room. My husband refused to come and see me that day when the doctor put me in the ambulance to hospital and I had to get a dilation and curettage.

The next day when it was time for my discharge from hospital, my husband did come to pick me up and his first words were to tell me he was leaving me and moving out and what he was taking with him. Two months later, I lost my job.

So in two months I lost my baby, my husband, my job and my sense of security. That is when the fear started. I became especially fearful of people getting close to me as I thought they were the ones who would hurt me. So I put up barriers, believing that was the way to protect myself from getting hurt again.

A long time later, I read 1 John 4:18 that says perfect love casts out fear. I realised that I hadn't been practising perfect love because if I had, there would have been no fear. What a challenge and what an impact that passage had on me.

I also learnt that there is no need to pray for the fear to go. Instead, I prayed for God's love to flow. It is an ongoing process, but I can verify that perfect love does cast out fear.

This was confirmed by a vision I received. Jesus and I were standing on what seemed like a very small island floating through space. It was very dark at the edges of the island – I couldn't see what was below. Jesus told me to jump off, but I was way too fearful. Then He showed me that over the edge, there was a light below and He was there waiting to catch me.

The message I received from that vision was that when I fall over the abyss, I need have no fear. Jesus (perfect love) is waiting to catch me whenever I fall.

HOW CAN WE LOVE?

How can we love, especially when it is someone we don't like or who has hurt us deeply?

Here are some steps that I have found helpful:

First, know that it is a commandment from God who loves you and wants the best for you, and commit yourself to obeying God.

Second, know that you can't do it yourself. We can only love by accessing God's love which is in our hearts through the Holy Spirit (Romans 5:5).

2 Timothy 1:7 says: "... the Spirit God gave us does not make us timid, but gives us power, love and self-discipline."

It is such a relief to know that we can't and are not expected to love in our own strength.

What we can do, though, is resolve not to be a barrier to God's love passing through us for the person. This is the process that we can be actively involved in, and it is making the decision to allow the Holy Spirit to take control of our actions.

Doing this involves identifying all blockages to God's love flowing through us. These blockages include any resentments, wounding, offence and unforgiveness. Share them one by one with God. He is someone safe you can talk to. Share the pain and all the reasons you struggle to forgive the person or persons. Then repent of each blockage and hand it all over to Him, thanking Him that you can and that He will take care of it. If this is too hard for you to do, ask God for help.

Pray for His love and forgiveness to flow through you for the person(s). For example, you can pray: "Dear Holy Spirit, would you please pour out your love for (name of the person or persons) through me."

Then listen to Him and be guided by Him.

You will know you are accessing God's love when you find yourself doing loving actions that you know you would never do if it weren't for God's love flowing through you. The evil one will attack again but just keep repeating the process. Eventually you will be set totally free.

God told me that love = power and power = love. God = love and power. The greatest weapon Christians have against Satan is love.

Chapter 13
THE WEAPON OF SIGNS AND WONDERS

The final weapon referred to in the words I received from the Holy Spirit was the weapon of signs and wonders.

Bible passages show us that signs and wonders make people pay attention. Acts 8:5-8, 13 is one example:

> Philip went down to a city in Samaria and proclaimed the Messiah there. When the crowds heard Philip and saw the signs he performed, they all paid close attention to what he said. For with shrieks, impure spirits came out of many, and many who were paralysed or lame were healed. So there was great joy in that city. Simon himself believed and was baptised. And he followed Philip everywhere, astonished by the great signs and miracles he saw.

Our God is a God of power. We have power through the Holy Spirit that is greater than the enemy's power.[10] Signs and wonders are a powerful evangelistic weapon because when people realise that it is God who is behind the signs and wonders, they want to know more, and as a result, many give their lives to the Lord.

---

10. 1 John 4:4 "… the one who is in you is greater than the one who is in the world."

Romans 14:17 tells us the kingdom of God is righteousness and peace and joy in the Holy Spirit.

By moving in the power of the Holy Spirit, we advance God's kingdom (1 Corinthians 4:20). For example, Jesus said that if He drove out demons by the Spirit of God, then the kingdom of God came upon that person (Luke 11:20).

Mike Endicott, in his book *The Blind Healer*, said:

> Our role is that of proclamation of the kingdom and then God does the healing as confirmation of what is being proclaimed. ... As we proclaim the good news of the character of Jesus and the outworking of the cross, then the Holy Spirit will come and confirm what we say with signs and wonders.

Mark 16:20 confirms that signs and wonders are God's witness to His Word. It states, "Then the disciples went out and preached everywhere, and the Lord worked with them and confirmed His Word by the signs that accompanied it."

Signs and wonders come in many forms. They include miraculous healings and people being set free from addictions. They also include receiving words of knowledge about a person that you have never met before and receiving prophecies about future events.

If you are a believer and willing to receive and ask, the Holy Spirit will give you supernatural gifts. Some of these gifts are listed in 1 Corinthians 12:8-10. They include the ability to receive words of knowledge and wisdom from God, the ability to communicate supernaturally with God through speaking in an unknown language, and the gifts of healing, faith and miracles.

Steve Thompson, in his book *You May All Prophesy*, said that when we understand that these gifts are empowerments provided by God to manifest His kingdom, our attitude towards them will change. No longer will they be seen as optional. They are divine empowerments to operate in the supernatural revelation and power of God.

The Bible says to ask and it will be given to you; seek and you will find; knock and the door will be opened to you.

> For everyone who asks receives; the one who seeks finds; and to the one who knocks, the door will be opened. Which of you, if your son asks for bread, will give him a stone? Or if he asks for a fish, will give him a snake? If you, then, though you are evil, know how to give good gifts to your children, how much more will your Father in heaven give good gifts to those who ask Him. (Matthew 7:8-11)

When I was prayed over to receive the gift of speaking in an unknown language with God (referred to as speaking in tongues), I began speaking strange words that didn't make sense. I started to panic, wondering if they were demonic. However, that is when I was reminded of the verse above, especially the words: "How much more will your Father in heaven give good gifts to those who ask Him." I confessed and gratefully received God's gift.

FAITH

We receive by faith and we grow ourselves and others in faith when we share the signs and wonders we receive.

Paul told the Ephesians that God's incomparably great power is for us who believe (Ephesians 1:19). To exercise God's power, therefore, we need to step out in faith. This means we need to believe that when we pray, we have the spiritual authority and power to see the result prayed for.

Remember, Jesus said in John 14:12: "Very truly I tell you, whoever believes in me will do the works I have been doing, and they will do even greater things than these, because I am going to the Father."

We need to embrace the words of 1 John 5:4-5 (TPT):

> You see, every child of God overcomes the world, for our faith is the victorious power that triumphs over the world. So who are the world conquerors, defeating its power? Those who believe that Jesus is the Son of God.

The more we step out in faith, the bolder we will get. It also helps to first step out with other people who have some experience in the area. For example, when I first started getting words of knowledge and visions for other people, I wasn't sure whether I should pass them on. However, a person who had a lot of experience in that area kept challenging me not to be fearful and to speak out the words. Now whenever I pray over a person, it is my expectation that I will receive words or a vision for them from the Holy Spirit and most of the time I do.

Stepping out in faith should be a joyous process and not something to be feared. Seeing God at work is actually an exhilarating experience.

This has been my experience and was illustrated to me in a vision where Jesus was leading a group of people (including me) up a hill. At the top of the hill was the most beautiful light. There was water a long way down. Jesus said, "Jump into the water joyously." And people did. There was no fear, just joy and fun. People did somersaults and flips on the way down. When I jumped, it was a wonderful experience. Jesus said to me afterwards, "That was a leap of faith!"

Exercising God's power in love is key and should be the only reason for exercising His power. When praying over someone, I recommend that we focus on them becoming aware of God's love for them. In doing so, we are handing over total control to God and then He will direct us what to do next. That is usually when I receive words of knowledge for the person or see the healing.

Having looked at the weapons of peace, love and signs and wonders, I wondered what others were available. I have highlighted the following in the next chapters: the weapons of perseverance, praise, and of sowing and reaping.

Chapter 14
THE WEAPON OF PERSEVERANCE

I was confessing some negative issues one morning, and in a vision my heavenly Father scooped me up and put me on His lap. He said, "Little one (I am always a child when I am on my heavenly Father's lap), you have so much to learn, but you are learning and I am well pleased with you."

I said it was so hard on earth coping with all the spiritual attacks, and He told me to *persevere* and let the love flow. He said, "Give everything to me and let the love flow."

It felt so safe and secure sitting in the lap of my heavenly Father, and what a vantage point! I could look out and see thousands of people in every direction bowing to God. I could see the seraphim flying overhead.

Later that day, I looked up what it means 'to persevere' and I found that it means continuing with an undertaking in spite of difficulty, opposition or discouragement and to remain steadfast in purpose.

The Bible says we are to welcome trials and tribulations because they produce perseverance. James 1:2-4 states:

> Consider it pure joy, my brothers and sisters, whenever you face trials of many kinds, because you know that the testing of your faith produces perseverance. Let

perseverance finish its work so that you may be mature and complete, not lacking anything.

WHY?

"Why" is one of my favourite words! And I really wanted to know why James said we should consider it pure joy to face trials because that wasn't my experience. In fact, I was quite happy to avoid trials if possible.

However, I learnt the reason is that trials and tribulations keep us humble and reveal our heart. This is revealed in Deuteronomy 8:2 where it says:

> Remember how the Lord your God led you all the way in the wilderness these forty years, to humble and test you in order to know what was in your heart, whether or not you would keep his commands.

Trials also grow our faith and test the genuineness of our faith. 1 Peter 1:3-7 states:

> Praise be to the God and Father of our Lord Jesus Christ! In his great mercy he has given us new birth into a living hope through the resurrection of Jesus Christ from the dead, and into an inheritance that can never perish, spoil or fade. This inheritance is kept in heaven for you, who through faith are shielded by God's power until the coming of the salvation that is ready to be revealed in the last time. In all this you greatly rejoice, though now for a little while you may have had to suffer grief in all kinds of trials. These have come so that the proven genuineness of your faith – of greater worth than gold, which perishes even

though refined by fire – may result in praise, glory and honour when Jesus Christ is revealed.

The Bible tells us we are blessed if we persevere. We become mature and complete, not lacking anything (James 1:4). The Christian life will be tested with traumas, disappointments, and more. However if we allow Him, God uses these experiences to mature us.

I believe God matures us here on earth because there is no opportunity for character development or maturity in heaven as there is no Satan there and no suffering.

The power of perseverance is that it creates a testimony in us and through us that everyone around us can see. When we go through a test, a testimony is always formed. What the enemy means for evil, the Lord turns into good.

HOW TO PERSEVERE

In order to persevere, we need to know that it is not what happens to us that is the issue, but rather how we handle what happens to us.

Jesus is our role model. Also, as believers we have the Holy Spirit always there ready to help and guide us through each of the trials.

Whatever situation you are in, cry out to God for help. Claim the promise in Romans 8:28. Remember, God knows what you are going through and He loves you. Ask Him to guide you in what to do. Hand Him your anguish, worries and concerns. Remember to give thanks and praise so that you can access His perfect peace and have His joy despite the circumstances. Reread this chapter so that you can be encouraged to persevere.

Paul said, "… do not lose heart. Though outwardly we are

wasting away, yet inwardly we are being renewed day by day. For our light and momentary troubles are achieving for us an eternal glory that far outweighs them all. So we fix our eyes not on what is seen, but on what is unseen, since what is seen is temporary, but what is unseen is eternal" (2 Corinthians 4:16-18).

Chapter 15
THE WEAPON OF PRAISE

The worship time in our church was building up to a crescendo. People were singing their hearts out. The worship team was giving everything. However I was seated with my eyes shut in a wonderful vision where once again I was a little girl sitting on my heavenly Father's lap. I watched with Him as thousands praised Jesus, singing, "All Hail Lord Jesus." I could see that it pleased my heavenly Father.

Did you know that we were created to praise God? In Isaiah 43:21, God says, "… the people I formed for myself that they may proclaim my praise."

Did you also know that we are commanded to praise God? I have listed in the footnote some of the verses in the Bible that tell us to praise Him.[11]

---

11. Romans 15:11 "Praise the Lord, all you Gentiles; / let all the peoples extol him." Psalm 150 "Praise the Lord. / Praise God in his sanctuary; praise him in his mighty heavens. / Praise him for his acts of power; praise him for his surpassing greatness. / Praise him with the sounding of the trumpet, praise him with the harp and lyre, / praise him with timbrel and dancing, praise him with the strings and pipe, / praise him with the clash of cymbals, praise him with resounding cymbals. / Let everything that has breath praise

Why do you think we are commanded to praise God? Is it because He desperately needs it? No. I believe the answer is because it benefits us. Praise is a weapon in that it gets our focus back on God.

When we focus on our circumstances, we can get quite discouraged. But when we praise God in the middle of our problems, our focus switches to Him and everything changes. It enables our mind to be governed by the Holy Spirit. We realise that God is in control and through Him all things are possible. It is all about focusing up towards God as opposed to down on our circumstances.

This is highlighted in the first six verses of Psalm 103 which is one of my favourite psalms:

> Praise the Lord, my soul;
>   all my inmost being, praise His holy name.
> Praise the Lord, my soul,
>   and forget not all His benefits –
> who forgives all your sins
>   and heals all your diseases,
> who redeems your life from the pit
>   and crowns you with love and compassion,
> who satisfies your desires with good things
>   so that your youth is renewed like the eagle's.

---

the Lord. / Praise the Lord." Jeremiah 20:13a "Sing to the Lord! / Give praise to the Lord!" Hebrews 13:15 "Through Jesus, therefore, let us continually offer to God a sacrifice of praise – the fruit of lips that openly profess his name."

> The Lord works righteousness
> and justice for all the oppressed.

WHAT IS PRAISE?

Generally, praise is lavishing encouragement upon someone for what they have accomplished; saying or writing good things about someone or something; or expressing approval.

Specifically, praising God is conscious admiration and thanks for who He is and what He has done for us. Thanksgiving is a form of praise.

PRAISE IS A WEAPON FOR SPIRITUAL WARFARE

Praising God is a weapon in that it gets our focus back on God and it is also a weapon in spiritual warfare. There are examples in the Bible of how praising God led to victory. Two of these examples are:

- Praise giving Jehoshaphat victory in battle – 2 Chronicles 20:22:

  > As they began to sing and praise, the Lord set ambushes against the men of Ammon and Moab and Mount Seir who were invading Judah, and they were defeated.

- When Paul and Silas praised after being beaten and thrown into jail, the result was their release, and the jailer and all his household being saved – Acts 16:25-34:

  > About midnight Paul and Silas were praying and singing hymns to God, and the other prisoners were listening to

them. Suddenly there was such a violent earthquake that the foundations of the prison were shaken. At once all the prison doors flew open, and everyone's chains came loose.

The jailer woke up, and when he saw the prison doors open, he drew his sword and was about to kill himself because he thought the prisoners had escaped. But Paul shouted, "Don't harm yourself! We are all here!"

The jailer called for lights, rushed in and fell trembling before Paul and Silas. He then brought them out and asked, "Sirs, what must I do to be saved?"

They replied, "Believe in the Lord Jesus, and you will be saved – you and your household." Then they spoke the word of the Lord to him and to all the others in his house. At that hour of the night the jailer took them and washed their wounds; then immediately he and all his household were baptised. The jailer brought them into his house and set a meal before them; he was filled with joy because he had come to believe in God – he and his whole household.

WE ACCESS JOY AND PEACE AND STRENGTH THROUGH PRAISE

Katherine Ruonala, in her book *From Wilderness to Wonders*, points out the truth that whatever we are going through, God's desire is to fill our hearts with joy and peace and hope (Romans 15:13).

We can access this joy and peace through praise. This is because God inhabits the praises of His people (Psalm 22:3 KJV) and in the presence of God we experience fullness of joy (Psalm 16:11).

So you can see that by praising God we access this joy. And the joy of the Lord is our strength (Nehemiah 8:10).

When praise incorporates thanksgiving we also access His peace:

> Do not be anxious about anything, but in every situation, by prayer and petition, with thanksgiving, present your requests to God. And the peace of God, which transcends all understanding, will guard your hearts and your minds in Christ Jesus. (Philippians 4:6-7)

Jesus showed us in the Lord's Prayer how to bring our requests to God. It is by sandwiching them in between two slices of praise. Start with praise, and end with praise. For example, "Our Father who art in heaven, Hallowed be thy name ... For thine is the kingdom, and the power, and the glory, forever."

We are told to give thanks in all circumstances (even bad ones). Why? Because it will give us peace. By giving thanks in all circumstances, we show that we are trusting in God and we can then claim the promise that in *all* things, God works for the good of those who love Him (Romans 8:28). Our praise becomes an expression of faith and a declaration of victory as we claim this promise.

Chapter 16
THE WEAPON OF SOWING AND REAPING

One morning, the Holy Spirit gave me these words of advice: "You need to get the focus off self in any form, e.g. selfishness, self-pity, self-righteousness. Get your focus back on God and off self and that is when the peace, joy, and love can start to flow."

God wants us to be focused on Him and not on our own selfish desires. This is actually for our benefit.

Galatians 5:19-21 (MSG) is pretty blunt about the kind of life that develops out of trying to get your own way all the time. It states you get:

> … repetitive, loveless, cheap sex; a stinking accumulation of mental and emotional garbage; frenzied and joyless grabs for happiness; trinket gods; magic-show religion; paranoid loneliness; cutthroat competition; all-consuming-yet-never-satisfied wants; a brutal temper; an impotence to love or be loved; divided homes and divided lives; small-minded and lopsided pursuits; and the vicious habit of depersonalising everyone into a rival.

The Bible tells us we reap what we sow. Galatians 6:7-8 says:

> Do not be deceived: God cannot be mocked. A man reaps what he sows. Whoever sows to please their flesh (their own selfish desires), from the flesh will reap destruction; whoever sows to please the Spirit (God), from the Spirit will reap eternal life.

I love The Passion Translation of the same verses:

> God will never be mocked! For what you plant will always be the very thing you harvest. The harvest you reap reveals the seed that was planted. If you plant the corrupt seeds of self-life into this natural realm, you can expect to experience a harvest of corruption. If you plant the good seeds of Spirit-life you will reap the beautiful fruits that grow from the everlasting life of the Spirit.

These verses begin with a warning that there is a law of reaping and sowing – you *will* reap what you sow.

You will reap *what* you sow. For farmers, this means if you plant wheat, you will reap wheat. For us, it means that if we sow resentment, that is what we will reap. If we sow love, we will reap love. If we sow blessing, we will reap blessing.

We need to be aware that the law of reaping and sowing is a weapon as it impacts on each one of us. We all have an influence and effect on people. Every day we are sowing through our actions and choices.

Jesus said, "Do not judge, and you will not be judged. Do not condemn, and you will not be condemned. Forgive, and you will be forgiven" (Luke 6:37).

You can see that in each case, what is sown – judgement, condemnation, forgiveness – is what will be reaped. If we want to reap a different harvest, we will have to sow differently. That means we have to change what we sow, not hope that the harvest will change instead.

Note also that we reap in proportion to what we sow. Whoever sows sparingly will also reap sparingly, and whoever sows generously will also reap generously (2 Corinthians 9:6).

Luke 6:38 says, "Give, and it will be given to you. A good measure, pressed down, shaken together and running over, will be poured into your lap. For with the measure you use, it will be measured to you."

The wonderful news, though, is that if we sow to please the Spirit, we reap the fruit of the Spirit which is love, joy, peace, patience, kindness, goodness, faithfulness, gentleness, and self-control.

Fruit is produced by sowing the seeds of that fruit. If these are what the Spirit produces, then wouldn't sowing to please the Spirit involve asking God on a daily basis to help us to sow love, kindness, patience, gentleness and so on in every situation we find ourselves in?

For example, if you are struggling with bitterness, resentment or anger, you can ask the Holy Spirit to sow the seed of His fruit in that situation.

Thank goodness, though, when we do fail, we don't need to wallow in condemnation because as we know, there is no condemnation for those who are in Christ Jesus. The way to move forward is to confess and repent when things go wrong and then get back in step with the Spirit.

The following Bible passage beautifully summarises all of the above:

It is absolutely clear that God has called you to a free life.

Just make sure that you don't use this freedom as an excuse to do whatever you want to do and destroy your freedom. Rather, use your freedom to serve one another in love; that's how freedom grows. For everything we know about God's Word is summed up in a single sentence: Love others as you love yourself. That's an act of true freedom. If you bite and ravage each other, watch out – in no time at all you will be annihilating each other, and where will your precious freedom be then?

My counsel is this: Live freely, animated and motivated by God's Spirit. Then you won't feed the compulsions of selfishness. For there is a root of sinful self-interest in us that is at odds with a free spirit, just as the free spirit is incompatible with selfishness.

These two ways of life are contrary to each other, so that you cannot live at times one way and at times another way according to how you feel on any given day. Why don't you choose to be led by the Spirit and so escape the erratic compulsions of a law-dominated existence?

But what happens when we live God's way? He brings gifts into our lives, much the same way that fruit appears in an orchard – things like affection for others, exuberance about life, serenity.

(Galatians 5:13-18; 22-23 MSG)

Chapter 17
OUR WORDS HAVE POWER

I was with my heavenly Father. I asked Him if there is the sense of touch in heaven. His response was, "Everything that is on earth is in heaven only better. My Word created earth. I have delegated authority to you. Your words create substance."

Our words create substance! This means we need to be very careful with what comes out of our mouths. Proverbs 18:21 (MSG) says: "Words kill, words give life; they're either poison or fruit – you choose."

WORDS CAN GIVE LIFE

Proverbs 18:21 tells us that words have the power of life. It is interesting to note that most of Jesus' miracles happened through His words. You have the power to speak life into people's situations and into your own. For example, you can say – "I forgive you", "You can do this", "I love you."

You can also speak life into situations using the Word of God (which is also the Sword of the Spirit – Ephesians 6:17). One way to do this is to speak out God's promises. For example, instead of saying, "I am always short of money," say, "The Lord is my shepherd; I lack nothing" (Psalm 23:1). Instead of saying, "I can't do this," say, "I can do all things through Christ who strengthens me."

I recommend finding out what God's Word says about your situation, believing it and declaring it so that you speak life into the situation. This is because:

- God's Word cannot return to Him empty (Isaiah 55:11)
- God has never broken His promises (1 Kings 8:56)
- It is impossible for God to lie (Hebrews 6:18); and
- All His promises are available to us today (2 Corinthians 1:20).

My favourite declaration is: "Thank you Lord that in all things you work for the good of those who love you" (Romans 8:28).

WORDS CAN KILL

I have always struggled with the children's rhyme that says, "Sticks and stones may break my bones, but words will never hurt me."

I don't think it is correct. In my experience, nasty words hurt. Proverbs 18:21 says words can kill, and there are several stories of people who have suicided because of words said to them or about them – especially through online bullying.

Also consider the words of Proverbs 12:18, "The words of the reckless pierce like swords, but the tongue of the wise brings healing." If words can pierce like a sword, you can understand how they can cause wounds and scars which remain.

We need to be very careful with the words we say about others. Also it is important to be very careful of words we say about ourselves. Proverbs 6:2 says we are snared with the words of our mouth. Our words have power, so why use them against ourselves?

Do you know someone who keeps saying everything always

goes wrong in his/her life? For example: "Everything always goes wrong for me!" "I never have enough money."

Be careful. If you say something bad is going to happen, often it does. For example, Job said that what he dreaded happened to him (Job 3:25).

Why use the power of your words against yourself and your loved ones? Wouldn't you rather be bringing life with your words? Remember, our words have power.

Chapter 18
Knowing God's Love

God loves us more than we can ever imagine and it has got nothing to do with whether we love Him back. He is love, so therefore love originates with Him.

Some people wonder how a loving God could allow horrible things to happen in this world. However, the horrible things happen because we live in a broken world currently under the control of the evil one (1 John 5:19).

God is in ultimate control, but until the return of Jesus, the evil one has control of this world and God has delegated authority to believers to bring the kingdom of heaven to earth. The terrible things that happen are not God's will for us. We must never judge God's love for us based on our circumstances.

It is the cross that is the symbol of God's love for us. While we were still sinners, Christ died for us. He died for us so that we could be saved and be given all the amazing gifts I have listed in earlier chapters.

The song with the words "Amazing love, how can it be that Thou my God should die for me" encapsulates His love for us.

God's love is also expressed beautifully in the passage below:

Arise, my dearest. Hurry, my darling.
  Come away with me!

> I have come as you have asked
> to draw you to my heart and lead you out.
> For now is the time, my beautiful one.
> The season has changed,
> the bondage of your barren winter has ended,
> and the season of hiding is over and gone.
> The rains have soaked the earth
> and left it bright with blossoming flowers.
> The season for singing and pruning the vines has
> arrived.
> I hear the cooing of doves in our land,
> filling the air with songs to awaken you
> and guide you forth.
> Can you not discern this new day of destiny
> breaking forth around you?
> The early signs of my purposes and plans
> are bursting forth.
> The budding vines of new life
> are now blooming everywhere.
> The fragrance of their flowers whispers,
> 'There is change in the air.'
> Arise, my love, my beautiful companion,
> and run with me to the higher place.
> For now is the time to arise and come away with me.
> For you are my dove, hidden in the split-open rock
> It was I who took you and hid you up high
> in the secret stairway of the sky.
> Let me see your radiant face and hear your sweet voice.
> How beautiful your eyes of worship
> and lovely your voice in prayer.
>
> (Song of Songs 2:10-14 TPT)

God's love is described as patient and kind. It keeps no record of wrongs. It always protects, always trusts, always hopes, and always perseveres. His love is not like human love which can vary depending on the circumstances and it is not conditional. He loves us whether we feel it or not.

When we realise all this, suddenly there is the most wonderful sensation of peace and rest. We accept we don't have to strive to be loved by God. We realise we are not condemned when we do something wrong – He still loves us.

Encountering God and experiencing His complete unconditional love will lead us to falling in love with Him. The more we are aware of God's love for us, the more we will love Him back.

Paul prayed this prayer:

> I pray that out of His glorious riches He may strengthen you with power through His Spirit in your inner being, so that Christ may dwell in your hearts through faith. And I pray that you, being rooted and established in love, may have power, together with all the Lord's holy people, to grasp how wide and long and high and deep is the love of Christ, and to know this love that surpasses knowledge – that you may be filled to the measure of all the fullness of God.
>
> Now to Him who is able to do immeasurably more than all we ask or imagine, according to His power that is at work within us, to Him be glory in the church and in Christ Jesus throughout all generations, for ever and ever! Amen.
>
> (Ephesians 3:16-21)

We can see from this passage that being filled with the fullness of God is a result of knowing how much He loves us. When we grasp how much God loves us and we become filled with the fullness of God, what follows is God doing immeasurably more than all we could ask or imagine, according to His power that works in us.

We live in a world which appears to be becoming increasingly dark. Light, however, always overcomes darkness and believers are called to be the light of the world (Matthew 5:14-16).

This was illustrated to me in a vision when I was with my heavenly Father in heaven sitting on His lap. We could both see planet Earth as a rotating ball. My heavenly Father reached out an arm and placed His finger on a spot on the planet and I could see a white spot which grew into an increasingly larger white circle. Then He did that for another spot on the planet with the same effect. He said, "That is my light spreading when people know my love."

Subsequently I received these words from the Holy Spirit: "This is not the time to be fearful or afraid but to rise up with the sword of the Spirit, trusting in me and my victory, wielding it and bringing light where previously there was darkness. Be bold and fearless, my loved ones. I am with you and will never forsake you."

The darker the world becomes, the brighter our light shines.

Knowing God's love changes everything.

www.ingramcontent.com/pod-product-compliance
Lightning Source LLC
Chambersburg PA
CBHW010244010526
44107CB00061B/2669